Right Wash
The Rise of the Patriots

David K. Kern

Copyright © 2024 David K. Kern

All rights reserved.

ISBN:9798342019040
Imprint: Independently published

DEDICATION

To all those striving to live and lead through a biblical worldview in our families, churches, military community, first responders, communities, and nation. To those holding firm to the faith without reserve or compromise. Continue running the race and remember the goal (Heb. 12:1-2). This book encourages you in this short venture of life that your pursuit has eternal value. Stand firm for God, Family, Country, and Truth (Lk. 9:26).

Unless otherwise stated, all scripture references will be from the
New International Version 2011.

CONTENTS

	Acknowledgments	i
	Preface	1
1	Bibles and Guns	4
2	The Rescue Business	8
3	Come Out of The Field's	15
4	Walk By Faith	19
5	Small Town USA	26
6	God Given Purpose	31
7	Ordinary People Doing Extraordinary Things	40
8	Certainty in Uncertain Times	48
9	The Battle	51
	Declaration of Independence	57
	The Bill of Rights	64
	The United States Constitution	67
	Bibliography	91

Right Wash: The Rise of the Patriots

ACKNOWLEDGMENTS

In an age of constant cultural changes and challenges, there is still only one truth that remains. This truth, when embraced, empowers us to withstand the ever-changing landscape of our culture. It's true; anyone who builds their life on this truth tends to be shamed and persecuted. A heartfelt thank you to those Christians who do not conform to achieve acceptance and survival in the world around us (Rom. 12:1-2). Thank you for your resilience and perseverance in an adverse culture. Continue to endure with strength and resilience, standing firm in a truth built on love, mercy, grace, and forgiveness.

PREFACE

Through prayer and preparation to embark on this journey, there was much time reading, meditating, praying, and hair-pulling to gather thoughts and revelations to achieve one common thematic identification. Page after page, line after line, research, commentary, and prayer again. The Lord mapped out the four main conclusive points. 1) Do not be ashamed of His Gospel, 2) Do not be ashamed of the truth of God's love for believers, 3) Do not be ashamed of the Truth of God's Righteous Wrath, 4) Do not be ashamed of God's righteous wrath coming for the unrighteous renegades.

(1 Pt. 2:8) states that Jesus is "The stone that makes people stumble and the Rock that makes them fall." This must be the awareness of the American church. We, as the American church, must stand on the Rock of Jesus, not stumble over the Lord's undeniable truth. The world will persecute us, the followers of truth, but we must remain determined and steadfast in our faith and love for God, our families, and our nation.

Standing firm on the foundational truth that sin deserves punishment, the only vindication we have from sin is what Christ accomplished on the cross. Shall we be ashamed of such a righteous display of love? That God, in all His manifold mercy, laid down His own life to rescue sinners from His inevitable wrath? We are not ashamed to publicly submit to the Gospel of Jesus Christ and our need for Him in our government. Those who openly and vehemently deny God's mercy will suffer His wrath. Still, for those who unashamedly embrace His mercy, there is a hopeful promise- the reward of eternal life free from punishment and wrath.

This is the matter for which this book is written. To encourage the people on the right into our civic roles to *right-wash* the stains of corruption, injustice, race division, perversion, and indoctrination that the left has imposed for many years. (Ecclesiastes 10:2) states, "The heart of the wise inclines to the right, but the heart of the fool to the left."

The scripture calibrates the reality in which we live: a left-leaning indoctrinated society that has knowingly and pridefully set itself up against God. Those on the right are waking up, seeing their evil plan fold out as if awakened from a deep sleep and rolled into a house fire. It is a time of urgency, a time for the "sleepers to awake rise from the dead that the light of Christ will shine on them." (Eph. 5:14). It is time for a Right Wash: For God, Family, and Country.

As our Forefathers submitted to God, so must we. It was through their dependence on Providence that we were blessed with this land. The pages of this book will implement scriptures that will define the path forward, including transcripts of the Declaration of Independence, the first ten Bill of Rights, and the United States Constitution. Today, there is much news surrounding the Twelfth and Fourteenth Amendments; it is encouraged to research these amendments for understanding.

Be sure to take some time to review the nation's sacred documents. This book would be a great addition to a small group setting. Take time to discuss the history of this nation and the documents that hold its fabric together. The reader will find that as the Bible and faith in the Lord guided our early founders to victory, we must not compromise and instead stand on the firm foundation of faith laid before us.

CHAPTER ONE
Bibles and Guns

Since the exit of G. Bush Jr., whose leadership at this point is questionable, there was an increase of assault not on the right-wing politicians who in every sense were Republicans in name only (RINO). The assault was pointed toward the average patriot. Obama's campaign was set on targeting the average right-wing American.

He labeled them as those who cling to their Bible and their guns, and he provoked them and instigated them. It would seem his rhetoric would invite losing his election bid, but it did not. The economy was tired under Bush, and the American right was coerced to support Bush Jr. because who else was there?

The nation was quickly ushered into war, inflation, and terrorism. All the blame fell on the average right-wing American. They were being jostled out of the bushes, no pun intended, to give an account of their leader. When, in all, there was no excuse for Bush. So, the right-wing average Joe was left to fight among the ash heap of corruption.

Obama capitalized on the feeling of abandonment, failure, and letdown; many from the right crossed over to the left to cast their vote for this man of color full of charisma; it didn't even matter if he carried the name of an enemy.

All the people wanted was change. Obama was received as if he was middle of the road on the economy, the sanctity of marriage, and abortion, only to transform our culture through his deception radically. I will never forget when the Whitehouse was illuminated in the Sodomite colors and sodomy was celebrated.

I stood firmly against Obama and supported J. Mcain. Again, this was the only force-fed choice, another placeholder for failure. I remember Obama's initiative of confrontation with those who opposed him and the party. The administration strategically placed operatives in the rural communities to go to the doors and provoke confrontation.

I remember one day, one of these operatives came knocking on the door; when I answered, I knew exactly who was at the door. I kindly told the man I was uninterested and not voting for Obama. He preceded to call me a racist and called my two toddlers blond-haired boys Nazis that don't deserve to live. I was not a Christian then, so a few choice words and warnings were communicated.

It was an unforgettable confrontation with the reality of the left's lunacy. More than that, I was serving in the Reserves; I questioned how could a possible Commander in Chief send one of his operatives to my door and say such horrific things about my children. Morale was down for many service members during this time. However, the excitement was up in the masses due to Obama's charisma and energy. A few years before, Osama Bin Laden stated that he would destroy America from within, and as it would be, the man with all the momentum carried the name Barrack Hussien Obama. There are no coincidences, only blind adaptation to believe the contrary.

People were promised they would not have to pay their mortgage; that was a wake-up; the economy shut down because people stopped contributing due to the promise of reset and free stuff. It never happened; the economy and the housing market all crashed. Some will blame it on political infighting, Bush, terrorism, or even chance. It is routinely evident that the economy crashed because people stopped paying their bills.

Obama was their coming messiah; he would fix everything and give it away for free. Instead, he was the infestation of the disease that would soon overtake America. He was the terror plant from within. People never had their mortgages paid. They were foreclosed on, and jobs were lost. For eight long years, people scrapped and clawed to exist under the dark cloud of leftist rule. The only ones who benefitted were the corrupt, the sodomites, and weapons of war stockholders.

The book's purpose is to present the experience of reliving these days. We must know where we came from to understand our choices about where we were and where we were going. We must realize that the left does not play by the same gentleman's handbook as the right.

In the Revolutionary War, the Patriots tried fighting the battle according to British law. The Patriots were getting walloped. It was not until the adoption of guerrilla warfare that the tide started turning. This was influenced by God's sovereignty and leaders who humbled themselves before the King of Heaven.

Does such a reflection suggest that there must be a call to war? No, but rather, patriots must better understand the weapons God makes available to them, "The weapons we fight with are not the weapons of the world. On the contrary, they have the divine power to demolish strongholds. We demolish arguments and every pretension that sets itself up against the knowledge of God, and we take captive every thought to make it obedient to Christ." (2 Cor. 10:4-5)

CHAPTER TWO
The Rescue Business

In my prayer time, before I left the office on the evening of November 1st, 2016, I knelt before the altar. Pleading with God for mercy on this nation, I proudly served this nation for what I thought it stood for; I recounted all the lives sacrificed for that same patriotic spirit, love of God, family, and country. In my prayer, tears streamed down my face, understanding the profound need for God's mercy on this nation.

In my time, I heard a voice speak to my heart, saying, "Trump wins." I have listened to God speak to me before, in the chambers of my heart; this was different because I came to find out hundreds of pastors heard the same voice. As I watched the election, right-wing and left-wing pundits had H. Clinton as the winner even before the votes were counted, but the voice I heard kept me glued to see the Lord work it all out.

The encouragement for this book came from an unexpected source. It was the early morning hours of November 2, 2016, the day after the fateful election of Donald Trump. The day prior, I spent the day in the church offices, completing my pastoral duties full of anxiety and sorrow at the thought of what this nation would become if H. Clinton won the election. I was up for the show from 7:00 pm until early morning. I witnessed miracles, and the hand of God swiftly moved, showing His mercy.

In the early morning hours of November 2, 2016, in the twilight state of rest, I heard the information from the news sources, casting news and live updates in the background of the miraculous victory. I heard Van Jones, with tears streaming down His face, stating that this election was a "Whitewash." Vehemently stating that this was a Nazi victory and that all people of color should run for the hills (emphasis added). However, I knew this was fake news hate rhetoric because I spent the year witnessing unity between blacks and whites in the figurative foxholes of faith.

I thought, "This guy has no clue what happened." This wasn't a "Whitewash." What just happened was a "Right Wash." This was a response to the eight long years of suffering under Obama. People of faith from every color had enough, and it was time for their voices to be heard.

I knew that Trump wasn't the savior. Still, I knew if he won the election, we would have at least four more years to right the ship, four more years to tell people of the dangers of what could have been if H. Clinton had won the election, four more years of provision to spread the Gospel without fear of persecution.

A few years prior, the IRS under the Obama Administration was pursuing Christian conservative organizations, and pastors in some states were being forced to turn in their sermons. The nation was in a downward spiral, and for Christians, the persecution would only increase. Trump won, and the risks and disease of our society, the leftist globalist ideologies, were kept at bay.

The moments of election night 2016 displayed what can happen when patriots, people of faith in Christ, unite against tyranny. The Patriots' mission and vision are color-blind. Yet, it is almost as if the left has such a perverse infatuation with diversity that it must project its judgment on those who don't pay any attention to a person's color. This thought process is incomprehensible to the left because their god and our God see people in a different light.

The patriot sees the beauty of the *natural* diversity of God's creation, seeing people's hearts as God sees. When the left sees only color or culture, they look for ways to divide, which stirs up hate and division because, well, that is what their god (satan) wants.

They want the people on the right to accept their man-made diversity of perversion and amoral inclusion; this is the case today because the wall of protection built around patriots in terms of unity in the righteousness of Christ

Jesus, regardless of color, is indestructible. They will never separate patriots based on color or Biblical values, so the left improvised and made boys want to be girls and girls want to be boys; they injected sexual attraction confusion into a cultural persuasion. They had men dressing up as women and reading books to kids, but whose kids were they? These kids were not the children of patriots but the left.

It is as if the leftist strategist concluded that they cannot separate Patriotic Christians based on skin color or unity in Christ. They, instead, invested in dividing the church based on gender identity, social justice, sexual choices, and politics. So, today is the rise of the sodomite culture (See Gen. 19 Sodom and Gomorrah), the sodomite banner waving in front of institutions masquerading as the church, having drags read stories to children; they have traded Bibles for relevance and money; these once beloved establishments of truth have traded truth for lies.

Through the sounding of the Trump-et, the Lord provoked the patriots to respond. It was time for God's people to wake up and exit their caves. The whole era of 2016 displayed God's mercy, grace, and, more than that, His relevance, power, and majesty to the right and left. The leftist influencers have sold their souls to the devil to be the mouthpiece of instability in exchange for fame and fortune and the vanity that comes with it.

Those ordinary people, the moderates, the sleepers working Monday-Friday 9-5, sleeping in on Sunday, who subject themselves to indulge in their toxic sound bites, are persuaded by the rhetoric of lost souls because they serve the same god or have no god at all in their minds.

What Van Jones saw as a "White Wash." People of faith of all colors saw the hand of God make possible what they deemed impossible, and the miracle was their curse. It was a "Right Wash," the rise of the patriots. Faithful patriotic men and women of all colors are pursuing a higher purpose. The leftists despise the purpose because this is a vision where the nation is governed by the rule of the God of Israel through His son, our Jewish Messiah, King Jesus.

The pursuit of (2 Chronicle 7:14) scares the living daylights out of the left; they growl and snarl at anything that sets itself up against their vision of amoral syncretism. They will go to the extremes of proverbial cannibalism, burning down cities, destroying businesses, murdering, removing law enforcement, or hypocritically using lawfare against those that oppose them. They have gone so far as to seduce and pervert the minds of their children and murder youth through abortion before they even have a chance to exit the womb. The left will use any means necessary to battle against the very threatening advances of righteousness.

They can't win, even if it seems they are. Their victories are their delusions; the Bible clearly states they will be on the outside looking in (Rev. 22:15), and the righteous will look upon their corpses (Is. 66:24). The Book of Revelation describes who the left is and what they can expect. Jesus instructs us through Peter that the gates of hell cannot endure or overcome the advances of the righteous, the church (Mt. 16:18).

For the tyrants to fall, they must enjoy the illusion of rise. This is God's grand plan; we must watch the left meander in their delusions and deceptions. We must strive not to be a party to their rhetoric or even, for that matter, get angry at their advances because, in all reality, their advances are their downfall and only affect those who think like them.

We are in an age where whoever is on the right will stay right, and left will be left; we see very few reports of those on the right crossing over to the left these days due to the radicle godless agenda that has been exposed. Historically, we witness and celebrate those who once were left crossing over to the right. This miracle is called a revival; the left diabolically sees it as a whitewash; however, let it be known as the unifying of people and color, *a Right Wash.*

I can say that I am a crossover, not a former

liberal nut by any means, but I did not fear God; I immersed myself in godlessness. But God! He is in the rescue business, and part of the duty of the *Right Wash* movement is to expose the deeds of the evil of the left in the public square, pull others from the fire, and save them (Jude 1:23, Eph. 5:11-20). This is the civic responsibility as patriotic Christians and a means by which we serve God, family, and country as The Lord rescues, so He calls His people to do the same (2 Tim. 4:18).

CHAPTER THREE
Come Out of The Field's

Before Samuel stood seven of Jesse's sons, all with the physical attributes of what a king should be in human understanding (1 Sam. 16). Yet the Lord rejected them all, and an eighth son was out working and minding his own business. A handsome boy, his stature was not in any way compared to his brothers, yet the stature of his heart was more significant than any of his brothers. The Lord said this is the one, anoint him, and Samuel did as was commanded; thus, at that moment, the Spirit of the Lord came powerfully over the anointed one. (1 Sam. 16: 6-7)

To thrive in the quest for relevance on a personal level, patriots must learn how to pray. Patriots must embrace how God answers prayer for His glory, realizing that there is a responsibility that comes with answered prayer, making sure God is getting the glory in return through the lessons of our forefathers. It seemed David was content in his work as a shepherd. David wasn't searching for relevancy; instead, he was the little guy of seven older brothers physically capable of anything. Samuel is sure that one of these seven masculine specimens was God's chosen successor to Saul's failed rule. They all missed the mark.

I can see young David in this moment when he was called. God often comes when one minds one's own business and is content in life the way it is, comfortable in their little people world surrounded by people trying to be big, the economic elites. This nation consists of two kinds of people: those caught in the vicious cycle in part of their quest for relevancy and people who count their blessings, do the work that is before them, are seen in the moments, and are thankful for the days.

David is the latter; David was happy out in the field. He was content and not part of the bullish quest for notoriety. Instead, He was thankful for what the Lord laid before him, and if one day it was something more, He loved the Lord, and because of His heart, he was ready. This is the heart of the Christian patriot wanting to live life and answer God's calls as they come, to navigate this gift of a life free from distractions and the world's contamination.

David didn't wake up this day saying, "Today I am going to be king." The thought didn't even cross his mind. When God called, he answered. David differed from the other personalities in the bible who argued with God and seemed to duck and cover anytime God spoke. David had tenacity. He was on fire, and outside of his flaws and failures, the spirit of God and David's heart for God were working in unison.

The servant David was anointed king by God; he was obedient and God-fearing. With all his heart, he served the tyrant king he was to replace, who was in emotional and mental distress because of his disobedience to God. David's music was the only thing that calmed the troubled King Saul. Even though David was anointed before his father and brothers, he was still called to serve them on the battlefield's front lines with the Philistines.

This little person with a mighty heart was about to shake things up, defeat giants when the big people were in fear, and declined to adorn the king's armor instead with a sling and a stone; little and mighty David saved a nation. He was laughed at, cursed, and taunted. Still, none mattered because David's heart was about God, the trust level was through the top, and David's relationship with God empowered him to do the impossible. Still, without seeking notoriety, people noticed God working through David and that David was one with God.

Samuels's anointing of David was just the groundwork; through adversity, trust, dependence, service, obedience, and patience, David would become king upon God's time in the story. Each of us is equipped with an anointing of the Holy Spirit to carry out the works commissioned by Jesus Christ. God is going to call His people when they least expect it. To be clear, He has already called; what will be the response? It is time for the Right, the patriots, to come out of the fields, "Beat plowshares into swords, and prune hooks into spears. Let the weakling say, "I am strong!" (Joel 3:10). God's purpose for restoration is a journey; the guide is the Bible. The power is His Holy Spirit.

What can be taken from the first part of David's story is his inseparable relationship with God, dancing before the ark of the covenant, and how that relationship led him into death-defying situations. David had abandoned himself in His passionate, persistent pursuit of a relationship with God. God wants patriots to have that kind of relationship because King Jesus showed how far he was willing to go on the cross; now it is time for patriots to stop putting limits on how far they will go for God and, like David, do it, the Lord is with us (Psalm 59). It is time to come out of the fields.

CHAPTER FOUR
Walk By Faith

David was anointed king by God through Samuel at the young age of 16. It would be over fifteen turbulent years before David would assume the throne God promised him. Over these 15 years, David was harassed and chased, had a hit out on him by Saul, his failed predecessor, and fought wars.

We know that David had a deep love for God, and it was his relationship with God that strengthened David to drive on through all the adversity he faced. His unwavering faith was the driving force behind his journey. Beginning in (2 Sam. 1), Saul dies, as does his son and David's close confidant, Johnathan.

After a battle of sides that is sure to take place after any change of power or loss of any magnitude, David is established on the throne as king over Israel. God then worked through David to defeat the Jebusites and conquer Jerusalem. We know today that this purpose was not meaningless but that through David's lower story, God's upper story was being told; we know today that that same city David conquered thousands of years ago is the Holy place of King Jesus' return (Rev. 21:10). Jerusalem the oldest city on earth has changed hands twenty-six times. Jerusalem has been a bed of conflict with Islam, the Jews, and, at one time, the Christians. Still today, Jerusalem is a hotbed for turmoil between Islam and Judaism.

When reading (2 Samuel 7:16), David's faith walk is extraordinary; through the line of David, God establishes his eternal throne in Christ Jesus. The last king to be anointed by the Almighty God is the immortal King, Jesus Christ. After finally receiving God's promise of the throne, David falls into a brief stint of idleness (2 Sam. 11:1). David, for the first time, experiences the wrath of the pride of a king. David decided for the first time that going to battle with his troops was unimportant and that he would stay behind.

With all the men gone protecting the kingdom, David was left in a hotbed of temptation. The truth is this… Being in God's will and moving forward in what patriots are supposed to do keeps them protected from doing what they are not supposed to do. That's what happened to the United States; the people of faith charged to preserve the land become idle—like abandoned houses. As the house sits, the years wear on the structure, and pests infest the structure.

Elections are a time for a *right washing*, but if right-leaning people are not up for the battle, as in the lessons we learned from David, the whole system is compromised. John Adams stated,

"Our Constitution was made only for a moral and religious people. It is wholly inadequate to the government of any other." If the nation's faithful patriots deny their duty to overwhelm the polls on election days, what more is to be expected than a total obliteration of the constitutional system?

The character profile of a patriot has one flaw that has sent this nation spinning toward leftist oblivion. This characteristic is both a quality and a flaw. Those on the right want to be left alone. They want a system that auto-syncs to their values so they can have less to worry about and more time to spend with their families. The responsibility of civics and church does not seem to fit into the equation of the lives of many on the right. In this regard, it is foolish to sit back and expect a fallen world to kneel before the principles and values of God.

It is reckless to assume that the same patriotism and faith that fills those on the right consumes everyone who considers themselves an American. It can now be concluded that this thought process and character flaw of the right has been the nation's demise. The church does not work without the oversight of faithful men committed to Christ; the same is true for our Constitutional structure. The Bible records the continuous fight for freedom. Jesus says that if the "Son sets you free, you will be free indeed," and the scriptures go on to teach, "Where the Spirit of the Lord is, there is Freedom." (Jn 8:36, 2 Cor. 3:17).

"So I say, walk by the Spirit, and you will not gratify the desires of the flesh." (Gal. 5:16). We know through David's lower story and his fall to adultery that working hands bring production and idle hands bring destruction. In the night's figurative heat, David was tempted by a bathing Bathsheba. Bathsheba was Uriah's wife, a soldier in David's army.

Uriah was doing what he was supposed to do, but David was not; David called to have Bathsheba brought to him; thus, the door opened, and sin entered; Bathsheba became pregnant, and David tried to cover his sin corruptibly (2 Samuel 11). Who was more of a king at this point, David or Uriah? David, who was now distracted by his sin to the level of covering it up, or Uriah, who longed to be with his men in battle and refused to lay with his wife.

This story has a familiar parallel; it wasn't until David admitted his wrong and confessed his sin that the restoration began, and the Kingdom continued to be established. It must be time for Patriots to cease trying to cover up the sin of idleness and corporately confess that the post was abandoned; the character flaws of those on the right created a pathway for the sinful left to compromise a God-fearing constitutional structure.

The churches have been ravaged by leftist ideology to the point where Bible-preaching churches are now the outcasts. The civic responsibility Christians were to manage was redirected through the term politics. The same church that led the way to victory through the Revolution has now been reduced to lowly attended echo chambers instead of Spiritual places of mass mobilization. In 2016, we saw encouragement about what can happen when people of faith stand together.

David was left in a battle he was sure to lose because he turned his back on the war he was supposed to be fighting. Thus, the struggle between flesh and Spirit raged, and Bathsheba was the first casualty. Others followed: Bathsheba, seduced by a king who was supposed to protect her; Uriah was murdered, Joab for carrying out the orders; the soldiers who perished along with Uriah; The baby who was conceived that died at birth.

Idleness is blinding in the fact that there is a tendency to forget that others will suffer because of the results of inaction. Yet, patriots must also embrace the truth that others will benefit from active obedience. David was contrite because of his actions; he could not fix what was already broken, yet in his relationship with God, he understood that discipline would result, but God would extend his mercy. (2 Sam. 12).

David's story is extraordinary because it is relatable. David's story reveals our faith walks, struggles with sin and temptation, a need for forgiveness and discipline, and God's mercy, forgiveness, and desire to restore. "The Lord is not slow in keeping his promise, as some understand slowness. Instead, he is patient with you, not wanting anyone to perish but everyone to come to repentance." (2 Peter 3:9).

We have all done things that deserve God's judgment; this truth will either push us farther from God or, as it did for David, pull us closer to the Lord. Our faith walks are also our stories of God's mercy, grace, and forgiveness. No matter what we have done or left undone, God will forgive if we contritely agree to our need for forgiveness.

There must be an expectancy of collateral damage. Still, with the embrace of the realization that this nation is under God, the Lord loves this land, patriots must get back up, love the Lord and steward the land, and intensely walk the walk of faith humble and full of resolve, seeking the Lord, and flooding the election booths while fulfilling the constitutional responsibility to public office (2 Chron. 7:14).

When patriots recite God Bless America and proclaim the Christian faith, they are responsible for more than they can imagine. These anthems are not merely patriotic melodies but declarations and oaths to preserve and protect this nation under God.

People are watching, and they are watching to see if we are committed to the leadership of King Jesus and whether our lives and actions agree. We will be noticed. Our lives are only strong when our lives and lips align.

The Lord has called patriots to be lights, to make disciples to be teachers, caregivers, pastors, encouragers, public servants, constitutional leaders, upholders of Truth and values, and vessels of His mercy. These are attributes of the patriotic right who led because they are led not by their ambitions but by the Truth and the Spirit of the one true God, King of all Jesus Christ.

CHAPTER FIVE
Small Town USA

I grew up in a small town; my father worked as a machinist, and my mother was an administrator. My friends and schoolmates shared a similar family structure in small-town America. This small town was a whole of brokenness from the stresses of life and demand. Unfortunately, in this nation, the small-town middle class is expected nothing more than to keep the nation's wheels turning.

Each purchase must be calculated, as the destruction of heavy debt was never too far away. Day after day as a child, it seemed it was a reoccurring event; fathers went off to work 8-12 hours a day, mothers worked or kept at home, and kids were sent off to school for 8 hours a day, pending they were not Latchkey kids who would spend 10 hours a day in school.

Day after day, the wheels kept turning as the government fat cats fed off the back of the average American family. Every four years, there was anticipation of a better future. Campaigns tugged at the heartstrings of the silent majority for their votes, making empty promises and asking the average American who was already strapped for cash to contribute monetarily to their campaigns to achieve the promise. Every four years were laden with the disappointment of empty promises, war, inflation, interest rate hikes, layoffs, and the rising cost of living.

The Bible teaches, "Do not put your trust in princes, in mortal men, who cannot save" (Ps. 146:3). The more significant issue here is not the leader but those who look to mere man to achieve salvation.

Every four years, the silent right begs someone to stand in the gap that only the Lord can fill. Yes, God uses men and women to achieve a greater purpose, but these men and women, as we read through the Bible, were dependent on God and God alone.

The patriot's mistake is that they idly sat by over generations, waiting for their mere man to do the heavy lifting. When that man was elected, they were proved only to be an asset and product of the system and not to their constituents. When we observe those men, everyone on the right threw their support behind them, and we will discover they were rich off the backs of the taxpayers.

A more in-depth analysis shows that only rich people can run for office, and the system has made this a reality. The patriotic middle class was never meant to excel, though one leak into their system occasionally only to be overwhelmed and later submit to the lobbyist control mechanism. Yet, we must delve deeper to discover that patriots have constantly been distracted by the bigger picture of government. Thus, they should have influenced their local government or colonies. They lack constitutional knowledge and become subject to the system manipulators.

The Constitution was written by farmers with pitchforks or men who clung to their Bibles and guns. During the Revolution, both men and women patriots united locally to unify over a more significant cause. The rise of the patriot began in the local church. It is where Peter Muhlenberg, on January 21, 1776, tore off his black robe after his sermon reciting (Ecc.3:8), wearing the Continental Army uniform. That day, Muhlenberg was responsible for recruiting 162 able-bodied Christian patriots; he led 300 out of the church into the 8th Virginia Regiment and later became a Brigadier General in George Washington's Army.

This is the left's fear, so they try to divide within communities and the church. Using social justice, sexualization, and open borders to exhaust small communities and divert attention from the greater purpose. Patriots have been distracted by the deception of D.C. That D.C. is the ground on which change occurs.

Within this mindset, the right has neglected its civic responsibilities to their localities. Thus, the liberal left has infiltrated city councils, school boards, positions of influence, and financial control. When patriots fix their momentum on the greater purpose, they will run for public office, take over school boards, be financial overseers, and build churches again as places of change and righteous influence. The Right Washing will advance nationwide when patriots advance the movement from within their communities.

I took the oath to defend the United States of America and the Constitution against all enemies, foreign and domestic. What amazes me today is that in my service, I was never mandated to or instructed on the Constitution I swore to give my life for. Growing up, it was as if the Constitution was a relic instead of the people's right to rule their government. Today, people have to fight through the web of manipulation and lies. The illusion that the government controls the people must be eradicated. The government does not control the people. The people rule over the government.

Undoubtedly, the Constitution was a gift from God to Christians. It was an answered prayer of the Puritans before us; it was a document written through the blood, sweat, and tears and the faith of visionaries who held these truths to be self-evident. Patriots must arise from their slumber, rip through the generational web of deception, and return to the fundamental values and tenacious efforts where this nation's victories began.

The art of war is to overtake without firing a shot. Throughout history, we see that war occurs not when there is the reality of the threat; war is the effort to extinguish the ingrained advance of the danger. War is the product of people awakening to the fact that the tactical and covert advances of the enemy have silently overtaken their land. War is the means to get back what has already been taken, to extinguish what has already been inflamed.

War is a fact of life in this fallen world. Yet, history shows patriots have God on their side. He fights the battle when there is confirmation that there is a battle to fight; with God, patriots can advance against any troop. The Lord is a warrior (Ps.18:29-33, Dt. 31:8, Ex 15:3). I believe taking our country back can be completed without firing a single shot if patriots unite and return to the fundamental truths and structure of our nation through the Constitutional rule of law through locally implementing our fundamental biblical values and faith in the local sector. Live local.

CHAPTER SIX
God Given Purpose

I had a great conversation with a former NFL football player. He shared his lifelong passion for playing professional football for his hometown team. Now, out of the thousands, maybe millions of kids playing football wishing the same, this dream became a reality for him. Yet he shared how his lifelong purpose felt meaningless when he stood out on the training camp field wearing his home team's NFL uniform. He stood there, looked around, and said, "Okay, now what?"

Finding himself farther from God in pursuing his destination, he shared how he surrendered that destination. Today, he is a director of a nationally renowned sports ministry and a pro sports chaplain. I have experienced the same standing there after achieving a personalized goal, then looking around and saying now what? How many have experienced empty, godless accomplishments? Solomon shares the same realization in (Ecc. 2:1-11).

One of the psychological assaults of the left is to distract people from a greater purpose: commercials, shopping malls, fast cars, Hollywood, and sports; all these advances of the left are meant to subject people to pursue fleeting and unfulfilling achievements. At first, they seem harmless, but it is not long before people pursue vanity as the world is falling apart. The Lord instructs in (Hag. 1:5-6), "Now this is what the Lord Almighty says: "Give careful thought to your ways. You have planted much but harvested little. You eat but never have enough. You drink but never have your fill. You put on clothes that are not warm. You earn wages only to put them in a purse with holes." The rise of the patriots must be a contradictory effort from the everyday world. The rise of the patriots will be a united front that puts off the world's distractions and strives to accomplish the greater good. The rise of the patriots will be a result of revival.

This assertion does not seem exciting because of the psychological uncertainty. The reward of transforming minds (Rms 12:1-2) helps focus on the fundamental objective. The Lord wants people to live in the fullness of his grace and protection; vanity instructs this is a tedious pursuit; thus, patriots strive to put those in office who will do the work for them so that they can go on pursuing vanity. The best person to fill a county seat, a school board position, a fiscal officer, etc., is the bible-toting, constitutionally literate, God-fearing patriot.

The Biblical Christian, the patriot, will not shrink from the call to fill the position because it is their life song. Nevertheless, each past is a haunting experience that diminishes confidence, especially when politicians expose the competition's dirty laundry during election season.

This is another psyop of the left, the deep state. That's why it is aired across networks. The character attacks cause those patriots to assess their past and protect their dirty laundry from exposure. Those on the left are not tied to a standard; they can be exposed for their immoralism, and no one expects anything less from the left because they have no moral compass to be accountable to.

However, a Christian patriot never wants to defend their faith or become a stain on their family; they are held to a standard that is the essence of their persecution and inaction. Patriots can learn a lesson from King David: instead of running from the past, embrace it.

Instead of pretending that they were born in a vacuum of Christianity, admit we were sinners, we were the worst of the kind, but God, through Jesus Christ, rescued us, washed us in His righteousness, and equipped each patriot for a more profound purpose. It is time for patriots to live with redemption on their sleeve, not only in Sunday's echo chambers but also in the public square. The nation is 100% full of broken people, sinners, and people with past.

Once patriots start exposing themselves and building their lives through transparency, the left has no grounds, and their threats or personal attacks will no longer be effective. Then, they are just left to attack a patriot's God-given values. Take J.D. Vance, for instance. He exposed his dirty laundry, nothing hidden; he used his past as a strength instead of a weakness, an asset.

His story makes him relatable to people; people see themselves in his story, and people are encouraged that if this poor boy from Ohio can become a senator and a vice-presidential candidate, any of us can. However, it takes hard work and transparency; each patriotic life is unique, and people are eager to hear these stories.

I strive to live my life through the value of transparency; I wrote about my story, *The Raw Truth Addicted and Redeemed*. People asked me why I was so eager to share my laundry to tell my story. Because unless we wear our redemption on our sleeves, we live a life in fear of exposure, why not expose ourselves to conquer the fear?

To many Christians, patriots live like the greatest do-gooder next to Jesus. They live their lives in the mask of perfection. This is a lack of humility and reverence for God. Yet, once we expose ourselves, we must stand up for what we know to be true. Yes, our God-given and constitutional values will be attacked, but our victory becomes even more possible when we focus more on offense than defense.

This leads to the message of losing our God-given purpose. (Ezra 1:1,3) "In the first year of Cyrus king of Persia, to fulfill the word of the Lord spoken by Jeremiah, the Lord moved the heart of Cyrus king of Persia to make a proclamation throughout his realm and also to put it in writing: Any of his people among you may go up to Jerusalem in Judah and build the temple of the Lord, the God of Israel, the God who is in Jerusalem, and may their God be with them."

Sixty years prior, Solomon's Temple was destroyed, and the Israelites were exiled from Jerusalem; now, God used a secular king to put into motion God's plan for his people to return to Jerusalem and reconstruct His temple. Not only that, King Cyrus provided all the means necessary, even the gold and silver looted by Nebuchadnezzar from the old temple.

In reading (Ezra 3), What seemed like a significant and favorable situation for the Israelites was anything but favorable in the region. Though they received favor from Persian King Cyrus, they were surrounded by antagonistic protesters and government officials who opposed the restructuring of the temple for fear of the rise of the dreaded God-centered Jewish government. Reluctantly, the Israelites tested their surroundings, reestablishing the Law of Moses, morning and evening sacrifices, and festivals. Upon laying the temple foundation, the

Israelites made music of praise and thanksgiving to God. An emotional outbreak of contrition, joy, and thankfulness overtook the celebration with shouts of "He is good. His love for Israel endures forever."(Ps. 136:1).

Then secular opposition struck full of bribes, corruption, and whatever effort could be manifested to frustrate the plans of the construction of the Temple (Ez. 4). God's purpose is never void of opposition. When I read this testimony, I saw that the comparison to our nation today is similar. When a nation has traveled so far from God and attempts to return to Him, opposition is fierce because of generations and organizations conceived of godlessness.

Instead of persevering in God's big plan to reconstruct His temple, the Israelites folded because the opposition was too significant; thus, they shrunk back into self-service (Hag. 1). There is considerable opposition to God's great purpose, the more critical the purpose, the louder the opposition.

Since the mid-1960s, patriots have been guilty of the same. They have shrunk back and built their own houses, worried about the internal rather than the external. Now, there is an increase in godlessness. In 2016, God-fearing patriots called out to God through a heart like Nehemiah's (Neh. 1:5-11). Miraculously, God answered. Will patriots shrink back to the lack of attention and care for the land for which God has made them stewards? Godlessness is throwing rocks at windows, spitting on us, and mainstream media perverting and demeaning the patriotic character and stances against gender choices, sodomy, abortion and our choices for leaders. Patriots are referred to as irredeemable, deplorable, weird, crazy, We the People cults, racists, nazis, homophobes, xenophobes, bigots, and many others.

These advances are a declaration of war on the character and values of patriots; it is a declaration of war on faith, freedom, goldy morals, and our nation. Patriots must not shrink again but must unite, stand up, and battle. There cannot be an avoidance of the apparent war that is taking place.

Patriots must wake up to the fact that this nation is at war and the patriot is the threat of the occupiers, the globalists. It is time for patriots to kneel before the throne of God above and ask for his anointing to go into this battle, to deny themselves, and to rise as good soldiers of Christ Jesus (2 Tm.2:3). It is time patriots no longer wait for someone else to make a difference. But they go and make a difference. "But I have raised you for this very purpose, that I might show you my power and that my name might be proclaimed in all the earth" (Exodus 9:16).

Our God-given purpose is to move forward as God-fearing patriotic soldiers of Christ, even in the face of persecution and oppression. The American patriot is not tolerated in the world because the American God-fearing patriot is the biggest threat to their advances. President Trump, in writing this, has miraculously survived two assassination attempts. If patriots wait for less opposition before advancing, there will never be movement of victory.

Each God-given individual purpose leads to one big reveal of God's great purpose. God's purpose is even more worthwhile if the opposition is thick. Do not be scared to stir the pot, do not shrink back, and stand for Christ, morality, family, community, and nation, even in the figurative and literal enemy fire.

The constitutional foundation, rooted in faith in Jesus, is crucial in our journey. However, how many patriots are not completing building the structure due to fear of oppression? Christ is calling patriots to His purpose. Jesus Christ, who came, died, and rose again, calls upon his righteous people to continue building from this foundation.

He says to Peter, "Upon this Rock, I build my church" (Mt. 16:18). The Lord did not say that upon this rock is the conclusion of my building. The Lord is building something miraculous. Allow Him to make His greater purpose through the constitutional structure He has provided. Fulfill His purpose, and fulfillment will come. This purpose cannot be lost. God's purpose will prevail no matter what, "The LORD Almighty has sworn, 'Surely, as I have planned so that it will be, and as I have purposed so that it will stand.'" (Is. 14:24). It is time to overwhelm our local and state governments, it is time to dominate the polls, it is time the world hears and sees the rising tidal wave of righteousness.

One nation under God indivisible with liberty and justice for all.

CHAPTER SEVEN
Ordinary People Doing Extraordinary Things

In reading the Bible, there is much to be learned from the record of Israel. Throughout the Old Testament record of Israel, it is observed that Israel is blessed and Israel is ungrateful, Israel rebels, Israel suffers, Israel cries out, God answers Israel, Israel receives mercy, Israel is restored, Israel is blessed, Israel thrives, Israel forgets, Israel ungrateful, Israel rebels, Israel suffers, Israel cries out, God answers Israel.

Though there is a personal relation to this cycle, there is also a national relation. Not getting too deep into the theological discussion, it is confirmed that America was founded by faithful men who relied on God's intervention against injustice. Yet, like Isreal, the history of the United States in her short life has displayed the same struggling characteristics as the nation of Israel did.

However, the truth is confirmed: "Blessed is the nation whose God is the Lord..." (Ps.33:12). God, no matter what, even in the worst kind of rebellion possible, when His people cry out, God's people receive His mercy (2 Chr. 7:14). What must be realized today is that discovering and experiencing God's mercy is a journey. God will not only provide a personal experience of mercy, but He will also display his mercy nationally, hence 2016.

Experiencing God's mercy is a process of lessons, and hard work follows to communicate and revere God's mercy. There must be a willingness to change (repent) continually. The Hierarchy of lives must align with Jesus Christ as the King. The trickle-down effect of God's mercy flows from Christ to individuals, family, work, friendships, community, states, and the nation.

(2 Cor. 4:1-2) states, "Therefore, since through God's mercy we have this ministry, we do not lose heart. Rather, we have renounced secret and shameful ways; we do not use deception, nor do we distort the word of God. On the contrary, by setting forth the truth, we commend ourselves to everyone's conscience in the sight of God." Each Christian has a civic responsibility; this truth has evaded the pulpit, as the tyrants strategically attempted and have been successful in deceiving the church that the church is accountable to a tax code rather than the truth.

It is as if the fallacy of *Separation of Church and State* works in their favor but is still used to control the purpose and effectiveness of the church. In return, what is achieved is a church that removes itself from its civic responsibility, preaches watered-down messages and publicly denies that the church has no obligation to civics. This strongly contradicts the ministry of King Jesus, the apostles, Martin Luther, the founding fathers, Dietrich Bonhoeffer, Martin Luther King, Billy Graham, and many other civically responsible Christians throughout the last two thousand years.

The ways and means God displays and works out His mercy are often shown through the acts of men and women who do not fear to stand against the narrative. In (Acts 4:12-13) we see ordinary men doing extraordinary things. In the halls of the ruling class, Pharisees specimens of the corruption of leadership; through ordinary men, they were left in Awe that these ordinary fishermen spoke with such authority.

The Lord uses ordinary people to do extraordinary acts time and time again throughout the complete biblical text and our nation's history. This truth plays out in Peter and John, Noah and their family, Abraham, and their family, Moses and his family, Joshua, and his family, Gideon and his family, and Deborah and Rahab, to name a few.

These were not excellent specimens of leadership; instead, they were ordinary people with life struggles. They came from a sketchy past, yet they were not disqualified. When God called them, they argued, they had low self-esteem, they were weak, and, like the average patriot, probably wanted to be left alone.

Yet God would have none of it; His people must answer when God calls. What we read about Israel's vicious cycle reminds us that there is a world with many voices crying out each day for God's mercy who are stuck in the same vicious cycle. As God sent Israel normal, average, boring individuals to be vessels and guides in the journey of His mercy, God has called the faithful patriots to the same task.

Many look around and conclude that more resources and people are needed before anything can be accomplished. Yet God reveals to us that Gideon, once in charge of 22,000 men, was reduced to 10,000 and then to 300 men to take on an Army of 200,000 thousand Midianites (Judges 6). Why? God says, "I will display my power and receive glory because, with a few, I will accomplish things that only God can achieve."

But God chooses the most loyal, passionate people. For Gideon, this number was 300; the Lord reduced the number and put Gideon in charge of defeating a nation with three hundred. The ratio was roughly 666:1. God took down a nation with 300 men. Would he not transform a community with 35? That means a church with 35 is responsible for a community of 25,000 individuals.

Israel was restored but again was retaken by

that same old vicious cycle. The personal quest translates into a national quest as a person's quest for the meaning of life; they try God for a bit, are blessed, and forget. People will go to a biblical church seeking answers; many will find these answers, but as soon as Monday rolls around, they forget their quest. Currently, there is a level of frustration in the church, which causes the church to become conforming instead of charging ahead. Many churches have instead put on the enemy's uniform.

Instead of becoming a guide to the Truth, ushering individuals out of the vicious cycle, many churches become casualties (Rev 2-3). When the church succumbs to the cycle, communities and the nation suffer. Instead of standing against the advances of godlessness, the church is distracted with keeping up with the change of godless culture to stay relevant. The only climate change to be considered in this nation today is the nation's relationship with Jesus and the tendency for many patriots to lose heart for the Lord and become idle, lukewarm, and ineffective.

Patriots must hold firm to the Gospel and not want to change it for what people think it should be. The gospel must be the staple of our vision and our being. The Gospel must be the lens by which the patriot vies the nation. The Gospel is able of both warning and commendation.

The world and those on the left would receive the gospel if directed only at commendation; the Gospel is rejected for its warning. Individuals cannot receive the commendation of the Gospel without fear of the warning, and the same goes for the nation.

The church's conformity has caused the decay in the United States. The Gospel is nationally confused among patriots; it has been removed from the public square, and pastors who should be mobilizing people into their civic responsibility refuse the notion that the church has a stake in politics. The result is that 15 million self-professed Christians don't vote; a significant number vote for leftist policies, ignoring the principles and values of God.

There must be earnest prayer for another awakening and a persistent pursuit of opportunities to engage civically, to profess Christ and the Gospel as it stands. Only Jesus Christ can bring us out of this vicious cycle. This will happen when Patriots unapologetically profess the Lord for who He is, the Savior of souls, the voice calling to repent to throw off the old (2 Cor. 5:17) and be willing to be transformed personally and nationally. God has called each faithful patriot to be that vessel of mercy that leads people to the Father, Truth, and mercy through love.

There is an individual awareness that the Lord

provides for us through Samson (Judges 13-16). Samson has the characteristics of pride; he is a guy blessed, but he takes the detour, forgets God gave him power, and loses his way. Sampson gets caught up in that vicious cycle of conformity, but in the end, the relationship God built with him prevails. It cost him his life, yet he was reconciled through confession and repentance, and what Samson did to that temple was the ultimate act of repentance.

Through the Lord, he brought the whole godless temple down on them. Imagine what the Lord will do with repentant, humbled patriots. The left's temple of godlessness must fall, but the Lord will only allow this when a people return to Him (2 Chron.7:14).

God displays his love for us in this way while we were rebels against God through our actions and inactions, thoughts, and speech. Christ, His only son, died for us, and when we realize we are caught up in the vicious cycle, all we must do is call to Him, and we will be saved (Rms.5:8).

There is undoubtedly a vicious cycle; this nation is deep in the mud and mire. Like quicksand, the more there is a fight to get out, the quicker the sinking. Patriots must come to realize the only answer, the only hand mighty enough to pull this nation out of this mess, is the hand of Jesus (Ps. 40:2-3).

Patriots must take a good, hard look in the

mirror and ask themselves how the Lord will use that ordinary patriot for His extraordinary purpose. We find this purpose in the terrain of public and civic engagement. The patriot's purpose is more significant than warming a pew on Sunday or cutting it up at church picnics; the purpose of the patriot is to be emboldened by the Holy Spirit to stand against tyranny and to stand against anything that sets itself up against God.

God-fearing Patriots must mobilize into their political landscape and crowd local government structures. The Lord is not going to give something that will not be valued. The heartfelt longing of patriots is to get this nation back, to usher in an age of returning to Jesus. In this case, there must be a strong call for repentance and to take back the United States one community, one state at a time, through the grace and mercy of God and ordinary people willing to do extraordinary things.

CHAPTER EIGHT
Certainty in Uncertain Times

God-fearing patriots are Christ's possession washed in his blood. With this truth comes a level of certainty that navigates through the perils of life. Yet, for many, there is the tendency to overlook this eternal certainty. The certainty of Christ is what this nation needs.

The reign of Christ as King is the fundamental certainty on which this nation was built. The assurance of God's love and His eternal plan for those who believe in Christ is interwoven in the nation's motto, "In God We Trust." This certainty is a beacon of hope in this season of uncertainty.

There is such an enamoring gratification in certainty. Waking up to work knowing the route one will take to get there, knowing when payday is, what's for dinner, what the plans are for the day, and what outcomes can be expected. Certainty engulfs humanity with a sense of peace of knowing and a little self-assurance that they have control.

Uncertainty is stressful when the road to work is closed, and there are rumors of layoffs and the threat of losing a payday. People wonder how food will get on the table, do not know what the plans for the day are, or are unsure of what the outcome will be. This world is uncertain.

As a pastor, I am confronted with many questions concerning these uncertainties, many of which I repeatedly replay in my thoughts. Because uncertainty and the fears and stress it causes people are valid, these are real concerns. At night, when I process the day, these questions center on one sure answer: Truth.

I answer these questions by using God's Truth through Jesus Christ and the Bible. Questions that revolve around uncertainty have only one answer, one truth, and provide us with the much-needed certainty in a season of uncertainty. Yes, there is certainty in a season of uncertainty and mystery, and all the mysteries of wisdom and knowledge are hidden in Christ (Col.2:2-3). Christ is this nation's certainty; when this nation forgets her King, the dark storms of uncertainty roar in.

Let the patriotic spirit be armored with the certainty of Christ, as this nation's forefathers covered themselves with the same certainty; they inherited victory. Certainty in Christ is the strength of the patriot movement. When patriots unify in this understanding, it is then that the greatest works of God are on display. Many neglect the biblical truth that Jesus is returning to earth to fix what humanity has broken. In this understanding, we find hope and reassurance, knowing that nothing is lost that cannot be found and nothing is broken that the Lord is unwilling to fix through Jesus.

Yet the divine secrets of advancement are not secrets at all. They are hidden in Christ (Col. 2:3). The secret to success in advancing the God-fearing patriotic movement is in Christ. Patriots must wear their redemption as soldiers wear their rank on their sleeves. Everything we need in strategy and planning is found only in Christ. Any other means to advance the cause will result in embarrassing failure. Nations who submitted to the God of Israel were the only successful movements on earth. Only in Christ is victory found and this nation be restored.

CHAPTER NINE
The Battle

In April 2020, I received an invitation to enter a live conference call to join other Pastors in the US to pray with President Trump, Mike Pence, and Franklin Graham. Without getting too far into the topics this day, the prayer was centered around an intimate petition to God for His hand to be on this nation and our churches.

Donald Trump's passion for the country could be felt through his tone. We are all flawed individuals, and on this day, I joined in prayer with a humble president and was blessed with the opportunity to join President Trump in prayer for this nation. It is a day other than the day of my salvation that I will never forget.

The results of this prayer are beginning to manifest, and the Day of the Lord is fast approaching. As the Day gets closer, the battles get more intense, and everyone with Jesus in their heart has a duty as good soldiers of Jesus Christ (2 Tm. 2:3). Assessing these current times, let's "Not be surprised at the fiery ordeals that have come and will come on us to test you" (1 Pt 4:12).

To realize the patriotic position of the battlefield, we must first understand the battlefield and the reality that the world, particularly this nation, is in a state of war.

WWIII is already activated. There is no turning back. The 2024 election is about choosing who will lead us through the rigors of war; let Christ lead him. It's time to wake from our slumber and embrace reality instead of running from it; yesterday is gone, but a better tomorrow will rise.

Here are a few forward observations regarding the state of the world and this nation. China and Russia have sent warships to the outskirts of US territorial waters. Ukraine and Russia are at war, Russia threatens NATO with retaliatory measures, and Israel is on alert daily, suffering rocket attacks from Iran, as they are bombing Lebanon. Protests are erupting around the globe against totalitarian governments, earthquakes, hurricanes, volcano eruptions, stolen elections, the bio war of COVID, heroin, fentanyl, invasion of US borders, abortion, perversion, child sex trafficking, gender confusion, and liberal indoctrination in the halls of public education.

Two failed assassination attempts on President Trump are sure to be tied to more profound ingrained acts of treason, lawfare, and J6 political prisoners. There is so much more; yes, we are at war. This war is ideological, spiritual, territorial, moral, political, and physical, and when the Holy Spirit lifts the veil, many will see this as WWIII.

Even though "Our battle is not against flesh

and blood, it is against the evil forces in the heavenly realms" (Eph. 6:12). These forces have taken over the bodies and souls of sociopathic power-hungry, money-grubbing elites that worship Baal, plot through their satanic worship in their secret societies, and spend billions upon billions of dollars to feed their war machine. Further, they turn hard-earned tax dollars and money that is spent on their products against Americans in this war.

In many ways, Patriots are stuck funding their efforts against the patriotic movement. How? Through Walmart, smartphones, Google, and pharmaceutical corporations. Patriots have ceased living locally and supporting their neighbors, the neighborhood grocery, butcher, and clothing store; what happened to them?

Americans put their fellow Americans out of business through the rise of government-regulated corporatism. Patriots were persuaded to their standards; the result is that Sundays are not Sundays. These godless funding centers are open on the most sacred days of this nation, and the result is evident. We now live in a land of godless carnage and morally rotted corruption, and the only way to restore is to repent and turn back to God and, love our neighbor again, live locally and naturally.

Jesus came to set the captives free through the truth; the question is, when set free, are patriots itching to return to captivity and disregard their neighbor because it's easier and more convenient? That's what the Israelites wanted to do; when the going got tough, they turned their backs on God. They yearned for captivity. The psychological analysis is astounding. What Egypt did to Israel is what the globalists have been doing to Americans. COVID unveiled Americans. Patriots realized they were slaves in a corrupted empire, and when asked for their freedom, the chains got a little tighter.

Americans were ordered to wear masks and stay in their homes; when the 2020 election was stolen, and patriots marched on the sacred ground and temple of the godless D.C. swamp, they were given more time in prison than most murderers and rapists. Unfortunately, they went without leadership.

Now that the left has been exposed, the threat has been identified, and what must be the patriotic response? Turn to the Lord and acknowledge Him, focusing on spiritual preparedness because God-fearing patriots are the enemy of the world. The fight is against a system that will be brought down by the very hand of the Almighty God (See Revelation 1-22).

Let patriots never forget that it is through the God of Peace that satan and his system will be crushed underfoot (Rms 16:20). So let patriots be ready for battle; things will get worse very soon before they get better, but that's good news when there is hope knowing how the story ends.

But for now, it's time to "Humble yourselves, therefore, under God's mighty hand, that he may lift you in due time. Cast all your anxiety on him because he cares for you. Be alert and of sober mind. Your enemy, the devil, prowls around like a roaring lion, looking for someone to devour. Resist him, standing firm in the faith, because you know that the family of believers throughout the world is undergoing the same kind of suffering. And the God of all grace, who called you to his eternal glory in Christ, after you have suffered a little while, will himself restore you and make you strong, firm, and steadfast." (1 Pt. 5:6-10).

There must be a return to the church, an overwhelming presence of patriots in bible preaching, and civically involved churches. There must be a united call to repentance and a united call to (Romans 12:2). There must be a unified return to the Lord (2 Chr. 7:14). There must be communication and urgency to overwhelm the polls during the election season.

The biggest fear is that the response to the Lord's answer prayer will be inaction. The Lord can and will pour his favor on those seeking Him. Yet, receiving the blessing is only the beginning. Patriots are called to be stewards of the blessing. Patriots cannot simply go back to the fields when elections go their way; they must continue to push forward, grow, and overwhelm the world with the Spirit of strength the Lord has given. "The Spirit God gave us does not make us timid, but gives us power, love, and self-discipline." (2 Tm. 1:7).

There must be an urgency to hold public office and embrace each patriot's civic responsibility. There must be an urgency to bankrupt the corporate means by which American people have been conditioned to exchange money for goods and transform this exchange of goods and services to the local level.

Patriots must wear their redemption on their sleeve, remembering that each election day is the day to rise to give this nation a good *Right Washing*. Choose goldy leaders, be goldy leaders, raise godly families, and build goldy communities (Mt. 28:18-20), and victory and sustainability of these victories will be close at hand. It is time to rise, patriots, rise. "Wake up, sleeper, rise from the dead, and Christ will shine on you." (Eph. 5:14)

Declaration of Independence: A Transcription

In Congress, July 4, 1776

The unanimous Declaration of the thirteen united States of America, When in the Course of human events, it becomes necessary for one people to dissolve the political bands which have connected them with another, and to assume among the powers of the earth, the separate and equal station to which the Laws of Nature and of Nature's God entitle them, a decent respect to the opinions of mankind requires that they should declare the causes which impel them to the separation.

We hold these truths to be self-evident, that all men are created equal, that they are endowed by their Creator with certain unalienable Rights, that among these are Life, Liberty and the pursuit of Happiness.--That to secure these rights, Governments are instituted among Men, deriving their just powers from the consent of the governed, --That whenever any Form of Government becomes destructive of these ends, it is the Right of the People to alter or to abolish it, and to institute new Government, laying its foundation on such principles and organizing its powers in such form, as to them shall seem most likely to effect their Safety and Happiness. Prudence, indeed, will dictate that Governments long established should not be changed for light and transient causes; and accordingly all experience hath shewn, that mankind are more disposed to suffer, while evils are sufferable, than to right themselves by abolishing the forms to which they are accustomed. But when a long train of abuses and usurpations, pursuing invariably the same Object evinces a design to reduce them under absolute Despotism, it is their right, it is their duty, to throw off such Government, and to provide new Guards for their future security.--Such has been the patient sufferance of these Colonies; and such is now the necessity which constrains them to alter their former Systems of Government. The history of the present King of Great Britain is a history of repeated injuries and usurpations, all having in direct object the establishment of an absolute Tyranny over these States. To prove this, let Facts be submitted to a candid world.

He has refused his Assent to Laws, the most wholesome and necessary for the public good.

He has forbidden his Governors to pass Laws of immediate and pressing importance, unless suspended in their operation till his Assent should be obtained; and when so suspended, he has utterly neglected to attend to them.

He has refused to pass other Laws for the

accommodation of large districts of people, unless those people would relinquish the right of Representation in the Legislature, a right inestimable to them and formidable to tyrants only.

He has called together legislative bodies at places unusual, uncomfortable, and distant from the depository of their public Records, for the sole purpose of fatiguing them into compliance with his measures.

He has dissolved Representative Houses repeatedly, for opposing with manly firmness his invasions on the rights of the people.

He has refused for a long time, after such dissolutions, to cause others to be elected; whereby the Legislative powers, incapable of Annihilation, have returned to the People at large for their exercise; the State remaining in the mean time exposed to all the dangers of invasion from without, and convulsions within.

He has endeavoured to prevent the population of these States; for that purpose obstructing the Laws for Naturalization of Foreigners; refusing to pass others to encourage their migrations hither, and raising the conditions of new Appropriations of Lands.

He has obstructed the Administration of Justice, by refusing his Assent to Laws for establishing Judiciary powers.

He has made Judges dependent on his Will

alone, for the tenure of their offices, and the amount and payment of their salaries.

He has erected a multitude of New Offices, and sent hither swarms of Officers to harrass our people, and eat out their substance.

He has kept among us, in times of peace, Standing Armies without the Consent of our legislatures.

He has affected to render the Military independent of and superior to the Civil power.

He has combined with others to subject us to a jurisdiction foreign to our constitution, and unacknowledged by our laws; giving his Assent to their Acts of pretended Legislation:

For Quartering large bodies of armed troops among us:

For protecting them, by a mock Trial, from punishment for any Murders which they should commit on the Inhabitants of these States:

For cutting off our Trade with all parts of the world:

For imposing Taxes on us without our Consent:

For depriving us in many cases, of the benefits of Trial by Jury:

For transporting us beyond Seas to be tried for pretended offences:

For abolishing the free System of English Laws in a neighbouring Province, establishing therein an Arbitrary government, and enlarging its Boundaries so as to render it at once an example and fit instrument for introducing the same absolute rule into these Colonies:

For taking away our Charters, abolishing our most valuable Laws, and altering fundamentally the Forms of our Governments:

For suspending our own Legislatures, and declaring themselves invested with power to legislate for us in all cases whatsoever.

He has abdicated Government here, by declaring us out of his Protection and waging War against us.

He has plundered our seas, ravaged our Coasts, burnt our towns, and destroyed the lives of our people.

He is at this time transporting large Armies of foreign Mercenaries to compleat the works of death, desolation and tyranny, already begun with circumstances of Cruelty & perfidy scarcely paralleled in the most barbarous ages, and totally unworthy the Head of a civilized nation.

He has constrained our fellow Citizens taken Captive on the high Seas to bear Arms against their Country, to become the executioners of their friends and Brethren, or to fall themselves by their Hands.

He has excited domestic insurrections amongst us, and has endeavoured to bring on the inhabitants of our frontiers, the merciless Indian Savages, whose known rule of warfare, is an undistinguished destruction of all ages, sexes and conditions.

In every stage of these Oppressions We have Petitioned for Redress in the most humble terms: Our repeated Petitions have been answered only by repeated injury. A Prince whose character is thus marked by every act which may define a Tyrant, is unfit to be the ruler of a free people.

Nor have We been wanting in attentions to our Brittish brethren. We have warned them from time to time of attempts by their legislature to extend an unwarrantable jurisdiction over us. We have reminded them of the circumstances of our emigration and settlement here. We have appealed to their native justice and magnanimity, and we have conjured them by the ties of our common kindred to disavow these usurpations, which, would inevitably interrupt our connections and correspondence. They too have been deaf to the voice of justice and of consanguinity. We must, therefore, acquiesce in the necessity, which denounces our Separation, and hold them, as we hold the rest of mankind, Enemies in War, in Peace Friends.

We, therefore, the Representatives of the united States of America, in General Congress, Assembled, appealing to the Supreme Judge of the world for the rectitude of our intentions, do, in the Name, and by Authority of the good People of these Colonies, solemnly publish and declare, That these United Colonies are, and of Right ought to be Free and Independent States; that they are Absolved from all Allegiance to the British Crown, and that all political connection between them and the State of Great Britain, is and ought to be totally dissolved; and that as Free and Independent States, they have full Power to levy War, conclude Peace, contract Alliances, establish Commerce, and to do all other Acts and Things which Independent States may of right do. And for the support of this Declaration, with a firm reliance on the protection of divine Providence, we mutually pledge to each other our Lives, our Fortunes and our sacred Honor.

Bill of Rights Amendments (1-10 of 27)

First Amendment
Congress shall make no law respecting an establishment of religion, or prohibiting the free exercise thereof; or abridging the freedom of speech, or of the press; or the right of the people peaceably to assemble, and to petition the government for a redress of grievances.

Second Amendment
A well-regulated militia, being necessary to the security of a free state, the right of the people to keep and bear arms, shall not be infringed.

Third Amendment
No soldier shall, in time of peace be quartered in any house, without the consent of the owner, nor in time of war, but in a manner to be prescribed by law.

Fourth Amendment
The right of the people to be secure in their persons, houses, papers, and effects, against unreasonable searches and seizures, shall not be violated, and no warrants shall issue, but upon probable cause, supported by oath or affirmation, and particularly describing the place to be searched, and the persons or things to be

seized.

Fifth Amendment
No person shall be held to answer for a capital, or otherwise infamous crime, unless on a presentment or indictment of a grand jury, except in cases arising in the land or naval forces, or in the militia, when in actual service in time of war or public danger; nor shall any person be subject for the same offense to be twice put in jeopardy of life or limb; nor shall be compelled in any criminal case to be a witness against himself, nor be deprived of life, liberty, or property, without due process of law; nor shall private property be taken for public use, without just compensation.

Sixth Amendment
In all criminal prosecutions, the accused shall enjoy the right to a speedy and public trial, by an impartial jury of the state and district wherein the crime shall have been committed, which district shall have been previously ascertained by law, and to be informed of the nature and cause of the accusation; to be confronted with the witnesses against him; to have compulsory process for obtaining witnesses in his favor, and to have the assistance of counsel for his defense.

Seventh Amendment

In suits at common law, where the value in controversy shall exceed twenty dollars, the right of trial by jury shall be preserved, and no fact tried by a jury, shall be otherwise reexamined in any court of the United States, than according to the rules of the common law.

Eighth Amendment

Excessive bail shall not be required, nor excessive fines imposed, nor cruel and unusual punishments inflicted.

Ninth Amendment

The enumeration in the Constitution, of certain rights, shall not be construed to deny or disparage others retained by the people.

Tenth Amendment

The powers not delegated to the United States by the Constitution, nor prohibited by it to the states, are reserved to the states respectively, or to the people.

The Constitution of the United States
A Transcription
(Amendments Underlined)

We the People of the United States, in Order to form a more perfect Union, establish Justice, insure domestic Tranquility, provide for the common defence, promote the general Welfare, and secure the Blessings of Liberty to ourselves and our Posterity, do ordain and establish this Constitution for the United States of America.

Article. I.

Section. 1.

All legislative Powers herein granted shall be vested in a Congress of the United States, which shall consist of a Senate and House of Representatives.

Section. 2.

The House of Representatives shall be composed of Members chosen every second Year by the People of the several States, and the Electors in each State shall have the Qualifications requisite for Electors of the most numerous Branch of the State Legislature.

No Person shall be a Representative who shall not have attained to the Age of twenty five Years, and been seven Years a Citizen of the United States, and who shall not, when elected, be an Inhabitant of that State in which he shall be chosen.

<u>Representatives and direct Taxes shall be apportioned among the several States which may be included within this Union, according to their respective Numbers, which shall be determined by adding to the whole Number of free Persons, including those bound to Service for a Term of Years, and excluding Indians not taxed, three fifths of all other Persons.</u> The actual Enumeration shall be made within three Years after the first Meeting of the Congress of the United States, and within every subsequent Term of ten Years, in such Manner as they shall by Law direct. The Number of Representatives shall not exceed one for every thirty Thousand, but each State shall have at Least one Representative; and until such enumeration shall be made, the State of New Hampshire shall be entitled to chuse three, Massachusetts eight, Rhode-Island and Providence Plantations one, Connecticut five, New-York six, New Jersey four, Pennsylvania eight, Delaware one, Maryland six, Virginia ten, North Carolina five, South Carolina five, and Georgia three.

When vacancies happen in the Representation from any State, the Executive Authority thereof shall issue Writs of Election to fill such Vacancies.

The House of Representatives shall chuse their Speaker and other Officers; and shall have the sole Power of Impeachment.

Section. 3.

The Senate of the United States shall be composed of two Senators from each State, <u>chosen by the Legislature</u> thereof, for six Years; and each Senator shall have one Vote.

Immediately after they shall be assembled in Consequence of the first Election, they shall be divided as equally as may be into three Classes. The Seats of the Senators of the first Class shall be vacated at the Expiration of the second Year, of the second Class at the Expiration of the fourth Year, and of the third Class at the Expiration of the sixth Year, so that one third may be chosen every second Year; <u>and if Vacancies happen by Resignation, or otherwise, during the Recess of the Legislature of any State, the Executive thereof may make temporary Appointments until the next Meeting of the Legislature, which shall then fill such Vacancies.</u>

No Person shall be a Senator who shall not have attained to the Age of thirty Years, and been nine Years a Citizen of the United States, and who shall not, when elected, be an Inhabitant of that State for which he shall be chosen.

The Vice President of the United States shall be President of the Senate, but shall have no Vote, unless they be equally divided.

The Senate shall chuse their other Officers, and also a President pro tempore, in the Absence of the Vice President, or when he shall exercise the Office of President of the United States.

The Senate shall have the sole Power to try all Impeachments. When sitting for that Purpose, they shall be on Oath or Affirmation. When the President of the United States is tried, the Chief Justice shall preside: And no Person shall be convicted without the Concurrence of two thirds of the Members present.

Judgment in Cases of Impeachment shall not extend further than to removal from Office, and disqualification to hold and enjoy any Office of honor, Trust or Profit under the United States: but the Party convicted shall nevertheless be liable and subject to Indictment, Trial, Judgment and Punishment, according to Law.

Section. 4.

The Times, Places and Manner of holding Elections for Senators and Representatives, shall be prescribed in each State by the Legislature thereof; but the Congress may at any time by Law make or alter such Regulations, except as to the Places of chusing Senators.

The Congress shall assemble at least once in every Year, and such Meeting shall be on <u>the first Monday in December</u>, unless they shall by Law appoint a different Day.

Section. 5.

Each House shall be the Judge of the Elections, Returns and Qualifications of its own

Members, and a Majority of each shall constitute a Quorum to do Business; but a smaller Number may adjourn from day to day, and may be authorized to compel the Attendance of absent Members, in such Manner, and under such Penalties as each House may provide.

Each House may determine the Rules of its Proceedings, punish its Members for disorderly Behaviour, and, with the Concurrence of two thirds, expel a Member.

Each House shall keep a Journal of its Proceedings, and from time to time publish the same, excepting such Parts as may in their Judgment require Secrecy; and the Yeas and Nays of the Members of either House on any question shall, at the Desire of one fifth of those Present, be entered on the Journal.

Neither House, during the Session of Congress, shall, without the Consent of the other, adjourn for more than three days, nor to any other Place than that in which the two Houses shall be sitting.

Section. 6.

The Senators and Representatives shall receive a Compensation for their Services, to be ascertained by Law, and paid out of the Treasury of the United States. They shall in all Cases, except Treason, Felony and Breach of the Peace, be privileged from Arrest during their Attendance at the Session of their respective

Houses, and in going to and returning from the same; and for any Speech or Debate in either House, they shall not be questioned in any other Place.

No Senator or Representative shall, during the Time for which he was elected, be appointed to any civil Office under the Authority of the United States, which shall have been created, or the Emoluments whereof shall have been encreased during such time; and no Person holding any Office under the United States, shall be a Member of either House during his Continuance in Office.

Section. 7.

All Bills for raising Revenue shall originate in the House of Representatives; but the Senate may propose or concur with Amendments as on other Bills.

Every Bill which shall have passed the House of Representatives and the Senate, shall, before it become a Law, be presented to the President of the United States; If he approve he shall sign it, but if not he shall return it, with his Objections to that House in which it shall have originated, who shall enter the Objections at large on their Journal, and proceed to reconsider it. If after such Reconsideration two thirds of that House shall agree to pass the Bill, it shall be sent, together with the Objections, to the other House, by which it shall likewise be reconsidered, and if approved by two thirds of that House, it shall become a Law. But in all such Cases the Votes of both Houses shall be determined by yeas and Nays, and the Names of the Persons voting for and against the Bill shall be entered on the Journal of each House respectively. If any Bill shall not be returned by the President within ten Days (Sundays excepted) after it shall have been presented to him, the Same shall be a Law, in like Manner as if he had signed it, unless the Congress by their Adjournment prevent its Return, in which Case it shall not be a Law.

Every Order, Resolution, or Vote to which the Concurrence of the Senate and House of Representatives may be necessary (except on a question of Adjournment) shall be presented to the President of the United States; and before the Same shall take Effect, shall be approved by him, or being disapproved by him, shall be repassed by two thirds of the Senate and House of Representatives, according to the Rules and Limitations prescribed in the Case of a Bill.

Section. 8.

The Congress shall have Power To lay and collect Taxes, Duties, Imposts and Excises, to pay the Debts and provide for the common Defence and general Welfare of the United States; but all Duties, Imposts and Excises shall be uniform throughout the United States;

To borrow Money on the credit of the United

States;

To regulate Commerce with foreign Nations, and among the several States, and with the Indian Tribes;

To establish an uniform Rule of Naturalization, and uniform Laws on the subject of Bankruptcies throughout the United States;

To coin Money, regulate the Value thereof, and of foreign Coin, and fix the Standard of Weights and Measures;

To provide for the Punishment of counterfeiting the Securities and current Coin of the United States;

To establish Post Offices and post Roads;

To promote the Progress of Science and useful Arts, by securing for limited Times to Authors and Inventors the exclusive Right to their respective Writings and Discoveries;

To constitute Tribunals inferior to the supreme Court;

To define and punish Piracies and Felonies committed on the high Seas, and Offences against the Law of Nations;

To declare War, grant Letters of Marque and Reprisal, and make Rules concerning Captures on Land and Water;

To raise and support Armies, but no Appropriation of Money to that Use shall be for a longer Term than two Years;

To provide and maintain a Navy;

To make Rules for the Government and Regulation of the land and naval Forces;

To provide for calling forth the Militia to execute the Laws of the Union, suppress Insurrections and repel Invasions;

To provide for organizing, arming, and disciplining, the Militia, and for governing such Part of them as may be employed in the Service of the United States, reserving to the States respectively, the Appointment of the Officers, and the Authority of training the Militia according to the discipline prescribed by Congress;

To exercise exclusive Legislation in all Cases whatsoever, over such District (not exceeding ten Miles square) as may, by Cession of particular States, and the Acceptance of Congress, become the Seat of the Government of the United States, and to exercise like Authority over all Places purchased by the Consent of the Legislature of the State in which the Same shall be, for the Erection of Forts, Magazines, Arsenals, dock-Yards, and other needful Buildings;—And

To make all Laws which shall be necessary and proper for carrying into Execution the foregoing Powers, and all other Powers vested by this Constitution in the Government of the United States, or in any Department or Officer thereof.

Section. 9.

The Migration or Importation of such

Persons as any of the States now existing shall think proper to admit, shall not be prohibited by the Congress prior to the Year one thousand eight hundred and eight, but a Tax or duty may be imposed on such Importation, not exceeding ten dollars for each Person.

The Privilege of the Writ of Habeas Corpus shall not be suspended, unless when in Cases of Rebellion or Invasion the public Safety may require it.

No Bill of Attainder or ex post facto Law shall be passed.

No Capitation, or other direct, Tax shall be laid, <u>unless in Proportion to the Census or enumeration herein before directed to be taken.</u>

No Tax or Duty shall be laid on Articles exported from any State.

No Preference shall be given by any Regulation of Commerce or Revenue to the Ports of one State over those of another: nor shall Vessels bound to, or from, one State, be obliged to enter, clear, or pay Duties in another.

No Money shall be drawn from the Treasury, but in Consequence of Appropriations made by Law; and a regular Statement and Account of the Receipts and Expenditures of all public Money shall be published from time to time.

No Title of Nobility shall be granted by the United States: And no Person holding any Office of Profit or Trust under them, shall, without the

Consent of the Congress, accept of any present, Emolument, Office, or Title, of any kind whatever, from any King, Prince, or foreign State.

Section. 10.

No State shall enter into any Treaty, Alliance, or Confederation; grant Letters of Marque and Reprisal; coin Money; emit Bills of Credit; make any Thing but gold and silver Coin a Tender in Payment of Debts; pass any Bill of Attainder, ex post facto Law, or Law impairing the Obligation of Contracts, or grant any Title of Nobility.

No State shall, without the Consent of the Congress, lay any Imposts or Duties on Imports or Exports, except what may be absolutely necessary for executing it's inspection Laws: and the net Produce of all Duties and Imposts, laid by any State on Imports or Exports, shall be for the Use of the Treasury of the United States; and all such Laws shall be subject to the Revision and Controul of the Congress.

No State shall, without the Consent of Congress, lay any Duty of Tonnage, keep Troops, or Ships of War in time of Peace, enter into any Agreement or Compact with another State, or with a foreign Power, or engage in War, unless actually invaded, or in such imminent Danger as will not admit of delay.

Article. II.

Section. 1.

The executive Power shall be vested in a President of the United States of America. He shall hold his Office during the Term of four Years, and, together with the Vice President, chosen for the same Term, be elected, as follows

Each State shall appoint, in such Manner as the Legislature thereof may direct, a Number of Electors, equal to the whole Number of Senators and Representatives to which the State may be entitled in the Congress: but no Senator or Representative, or Person holding an Office of Trust or Profit under the United States, shall be appointed an Elector.

<u>The Electors shall meet in their respective States, and vote by Ballot for two Persons, of whom one at least shall not be an Inhabitant of the same State with themselves. And they shall make a List of all the Persons voted for, and of the Number of Votes for each; which List they shall sign and certify, and transmit sealed to the Seat of the Government of the United States, directed to the President of the Senate. The President of the Senate shall, in the Presence of the Senate and House of Representatives, open all the Certificates, and the Votes shall then be counted. The Person having the greatest Number of Votes shall be the President, if such Number be a Majority of the whole Number of Electors appointed; and if there be more than one who have such Majority, and have an equal</u>

Number of Votes, then the House of Representatives shall immediately chuse by Ballot one of them for President; and if no Person have a Majority, then from the five highest on the List the said House shall in like Manner chuse the President. But in chusing the President, the Votes shall be taken by States, the Representation from each State having one Vote; A quorum for this Purpose shall consist of a Member or Members from two thirds of the States, and a Majority of all the States shall be necessary to a Choice. In every Case, after the Choice of the President, the Person having the greatest Number of Votes of the Electors shall be the Vice President. But if there should remain two or more who have equal Votes, the Senate shall chuse from them by Ballot the Vice President.

The Congress may determine the Time of chusing the Electors, and the Day on which they shall give their Votes; which Day shall be the same throughout the United States.

No Person except a natural born Citizen, or a Citizen of the United States, at the time of the Adoption of this Constitution, shall be eligible to the Office of President; neither shall any Person be eligible to that Office who shall not have attained to the Age of thirty five Years, and been fourteen Years a Resident within the United States.

<u>In Case of the Removal of the President from Office, or of his Death, Resignation, or Inability to discharge the Powers and Duties of the said Office, the Same shall devolve on the Vice President, and the Congress may by Law provide for the Case of Removal, Death, Resignation or Inability, both of the President and Vice President, declaring what Officer shall then act as President, and such Officer shall act accordingly, until the Disability be removed, or a President shall be elected.</u>

The President shall, at stated Times, receive for his Services, a Compensation, which shall neither be encreased nor diminished during the Period for which he shall have been elected, and he shall not receive within that Period any other Emolument from the United States, or any of them.

Before he enter on the Execution of his Office, he shall take the following Oath or Affirmation:—"I do solemnly swear (or affirm) that I will faithfully execute the Office of President of the United States, and will to the best of my Ability, preserve, protect and defend the Constitution of the United States."

Section. 2.

The President shall be Commander in Chief of the Army and Navy of the United States, and of the Militia of the several States, when called into the actual Service of the United States; he may require the Opinion, in writing, of the principal Officer in each of the executive Departments, upon any Subject relating to the Duties of their respective Offices, and he shall have Power to grant Reprieves and Pardons for Offences against the United States, except in Cases of Impeachment.

He shall have Power, by and with the Advice and Consent of the Senate, to make Treaties, provided two thirds of the Senators present concur; and he shall nominate, and by and with the Advice and Consent of the Senate, shall appoint Ambassadors, other public Ministers and Consuls, Judges of the supreme Court, and all other Officers of the United States, whose Appointments are not herein otherwise provided for, and which shall be established by Law: but the Congress may by Law vest the Appointment of such inferior Officers, as they think proper, in the President alone, in the Courts of Law, or in the Heads of Departments.

The President shall have Power to fill up all Vacancies that may happen during the Recess of the Senate, by granting Commissions which shall expire at the End of their next Session.

Section. 3.

He shall from time to time give to the Congress Information of the State of the Union, and recommend to their Consideration such Measures as he shall judge necessary and expedient; he may, on extraordinary Occasions, convene both Houses, or either of them, and in Case of Disagreement between them, with Respect to the Time of Adjournment, he may adjourn them to such Time as he shall think proper; he shall receive Ambassadors and other public Ministers; he shall take Care that the Laws be faithfully executed, and shall Commission all the Officers of the United States.

Section. 4.

The President, Vice President and all civil Officers of the United States, shall be removed from Office on Impeachment for, and Conviction of, Treason, Bribery, or other high Crimes and Misdemeanors.

Article. III.

Section. 1.

The judicial Power of the United States, shall be vested in one supreme Court, and in such inferior Courts as the Congress may from time to time ordain and establish. The Judges, both of the supreme and inferior Courts, shall hold their Offices during good Behaviour, and shall, at stated Times, receive for their Services, a Compensation, which shall not be diminished during their Continuance in Office.

Section. 2.

The judicial Power shall extend to all Cases, in Law and Equity, arising under this Constitution, the Laws of the United States, and Treaties made, or which shall be made, under their Authority;—to all Cases affecting Ambassadors, other public Ministers and Consuls;—to all Cases of admiralty and maritime Jurisdiction;—to Controversies to which the United States shall be a Party;—to Controversies between two or more States;— <u>between a State and Citizens of another State</u>,—between Citizens of different States,—between Citizens of the same State claiming Lands under Grants of different States, and between a State, or the Citizens thereof, and foreign States, Citizens or Subjects.

In all Cases affecting Ambassadors, other public Ministers and Consuls, and those in which a State shall be Party, the supreme Court shall have original Jurisdiction. In all the other Cases before mentioned, the supreme Court shall have appellate Jurisdiction, both as to Law and Fact, with such Exceptions, and under such Regulations as the Congress shall make.

The Trial of all Crimes, except in Cases of Impeachment, shall be by Jury; and such Trial shall be held in the State where the said Crimes shall have been committed; but when not committed within any State, the Trial shall be at such Place or Places as the Congress may by Law have directed.

Section. 3.

Treason against the United States, shall consist only in levying War against them, or in adhering to their Enemies, giving them Aid and Comfort. No Person shall be convicted of Treason unless on the Testimony of two Witnesses to the same overt Act, or on Confession in open Court.

The Congress shall have Power to declare the Punishment of Treason, but no Attainder of Treason shall work Corruption of Blood, or Forfeiture except during the Life of the Person attainted.

Article. IV.

Section. 1.

Full Faith and Credit shall be given in each State to the public Acts, Records, and judicial Proceedings of every other State. And the Congress may by general Laws prescribe the Manner in which such Acts, Records and Proceedings shall be proved, and the Effect thereof.

Section. 2.

The Citizens of each State shall be entitled to all Privileges and Immunities of Citizens in the several States.

A Person charged in any State with Treason, Felony, or other Crime, who shall flee from Justice, and be found in another State, shall on Demand of the executive Authority of the State from which he fled, be delivered up, to be removed to the State having Jurisdiction of the Crime.

<u>No Person held to Service or Labour in one State, under the Laws thereof, escaping into another, shall, in Consequence of any Law or Regulation therein, be discharged from such Service or Labour, but shall be delivered up on Claim of the Party to whom such Service or Labour may be due.</u>

Section. 3.

New States may be admitted by the Congress into this Union; but no new State shall be formed or erected within the Jurisdiction of any other State; nor any State be formed by the Junction of two or more States, or Parts of States, without the Consent of the Legislatures of the States concerned as well as of the Congress.

The Congress shall have Power to dispose of and make all needful Rules and Regulations respecting the Territory or other Property belonging to the United States; and nothing in this Constitution shall be so construed as to Prejudice any Claims of the United States, or of any particular State.

Section. 4.

The United States shall guarantee to every State in this Union a Republican Form of Government, and shall protect each of them against Invasion; and on Application of the Legislature, or of the Executive (when the Legislature cannot be convened) against domestic Violence.

Article. V.

The Congress, whenever two thirds of both Houses shall deem it necessary, shall propose Amendments to this Constitution, or, on the Application of the Legislatures of two thirds of the several States, shall call a Convention for proposing Amendments, which, in either Case, shall be valid to all Intents and Purposes, as Part of this Constitution, when ratified by the Legislatures of three fourths of the several States, or by Conventions in three fourths thereof, as the one or the other Mode of Ratification may be proposed by the Congress; Provided that no Amendment which may be made prior to the Year One thousand eight hundred and eight shall in any Manner affect the first and fourth Clauses in the Ninth Section of the first Article; and that no State, without its Consent, shall be deprived of its equal Suffrage in the Senate.

Article. VI.

All Debts contracted and Engagements entered into, before the Adoption of this Constitution, shall be as valid against the United States under this Constitution, as under the Confederation.

This Constitution, and the Laws of the United States which shall be made in Pursuance thereof; and all Treaties made, or which shall be made, under the Authority of the United States, shall be the supreme Law of the Land; and the Judges in every State shall be bound thereby, any Thing in the Constitution or Laws of any State to the Contrary notwithstanding.

The Senators and Representatives before mentioned, and the Members of the several State Legislatures, and all executive and judicial Officers, both of the United States and of the several States, shall be bound by Oath or Affirmation, to support this Constitution; but no religious Test shall ever be required as a Qualification to any Office or public Trust under the United States.

Article. VII.

The Ratification of the Conventions of nine States, shall be sufficient for the Establishment of this Constitution between the States so ratifying the Same.

The Word, "the," being interlined between the seventh and eighth Lines of the first Page, The Word "Thirty" being partly written on an Erazure in the fifteenth Line of the first Page, The Words "is tried" being interlined between the thirty second and thirty third Lines of the first Page and the Word "the" being interlined between the forty third and forty fourth Lines of the second Page.

Attest William Jackson Secretary

done in Convention by the Unanimous Consent of the States present the Seventeenth Day of September in the Year of our Lord one thousand seven hundred and Eighty seven and of the Independance of the United States of America the Twelfth In witness whereof We have hereunto subscribed our Names,

G°. Washington
President and deputy from Virginia

> Delaware
> Geo: Read
> Gunning Bedford jun
> John Dickinson
> Richard Bassett
> Jaco: Broom
>
> Maryland
> James McHenry
> Dan of St Thos. Jenifer
> Danl. Carroll
>
> Virginia
> John Blair
> James Madison Jr.
>
> North Carolina
> Wm. Blount
> Richd. Dobbs Spaight
> Hu Williamson
>
> South Carolina

J. Rutledge
Charles Cotesworth Pinckney
Charles Pinckney
Pierce Butler

<u>Georgia</u>
William Few
Abr Baldwin

<u>New Hampshire</u>
John Langdon
Nicholas Gilman

<u>Massachusetts</u>
Nathaniel Gorham
Rufus King

<u>Connecticut</u>
Wm. Saml. Johnson
Roger Sherman

<u>New York</u>
Alexander Hamilton

<u>New Jersey</u>
Wil: Livingston
David Brearley
Wm. Paterson
Jona: Dayton

<u>Pennsylvania</u>
B Franklin
Thomas Mifflin
Robt. Morris
Geo. Clymer
Thos. FitzSimons
Jared Ingersoll
James Wilson
Gouv Morris

BIBLIOGRAPHY

National Archives . (2024, August 24). *Americas Founding Documents* . Retrieved from National Archives : https://www.archives.gov/founding-docs/declaration-transcript

National Archives. (2021, December 21). *Americas Founding Documents.* Retrieved from https://www.archives.gov/founding-docs/constitution: https://www.archives.gov/founding-docs/constitution

Wikipedia contributors. (2024, August 5). *The Free Encyclopedia.* Retrieved from Wikipedia: https://en.wikipedia.org/w/index.php?title=Peter_Muhlenberg&oldid=1238746653

ABOUT THE AUTHOR

Right Wash: Rise of the Patriots is David's second book. David previously published a story about his life in the book The Raw Truth Addicted and Redeemed. David lives in Northeast Ohio with his beautiful wife, Ronda, and they have three lovely adult children. David is the senior pastor of Vitality Church. David serves in various civic roles and is passionate about the Lord's word, love of country, and boldly professing Truth in the public square.

Made in the USA
Monee, IL
26 October 2024